IN MY HEAD, ON MY MIND

ABOUT THE AUTHOR

Christopher Cousins was born in Brighton, East Sussex, in 1934. He grew up in Bognor Regis, West Sussex, where he attended Nyewood Lane C of E Primary School. This was where his interest in reading poetry began, further encouraged at home by his mother.

In September 1945 he started at Midhurst Grammar School, West Sussex, but in October the family moved to Chelsea, SW London. Not wishing to abandon his new school he became a boarder in term time. There his interest in poetry extended to writing it. And so it continued through National Service in the RAF (1953-55), through student days reading Physics at Keble College, Oxford (1955-58), into marriage (1958), fatherhood and employment: teaching physics at Radley College (1959-61) and at Taunton's School, Southampton (1962-64).

He was appointed to the staff of the Physics Department at Exeter University in 1964 and simultaneously his interest in poetry went to sleep. He took Early Retirement in 1990 and since then has enjoyed a number of Creative Writing courses and workshops with Exeter University, the Arvon Foundation, the Poetry School, the WEA and Plymouth University from whom he obtained his MA in 2004 with a dissertation on *Science & Poetry and a Collection of Poems*.

His first volume, *Remembering How It Was*, focuses on events in the '40s, '50s and early '60s.

In My Head, On My Mind

Christopher Cousins

CreateSpace

Independent Publishing Platform

2015

First published in 2015
by CreateSpace Independent Publishing Platform

Typeface: Palatino

All rights reserved
© Christopher Cousins, 2015

The right of Christopher Cousins to be identified as author of this work has been asserted in accordance with Section 77 of the Copyright, Designs and Patents Act 1988

ISBN-13: 978 - 1512080070

ISBN-10: 1512080071

CREDO

The scientific method has expanded our understanding of life and the universe in spectacular fashion across the entire scale of space and time, in every sensory modality, and beyond the farthest dreams of the pre-scientific mind.

All of experience is still processed by the sensory and nervous systems peculiar to our species, and all of knowledge is still evaluated by our idiosyncratically evolved emotions.

Both the research scientist and the creative writer are members of *Homo sapiens*, in the family *Hominidæ* of the order *Primates*, and a biological species exquisitely adapted to planet Earth.

Art is in our bones: we all live by narrative and metaphor.

> E. O. Wilson in *Wings across two cultures*.

THANKS

... firstly to Andrew Hoellering for introducing me to the self-publishing website, CreateSpace, and for suggesting that I publish my poems through them. This collection is the second of two that have resulted.

... to the lecturers who contributed the Creative Writing modules to the Integrated Masters Programme of the University of Plymouth. In particular Tony Lopez whose *Poetry* module was both challenging and inspiring, represented here by *Ann's Song*, and whose supervision of my MA dissertation on *Science & Poetry, and a Collection of Poems* was enthusiastic and diligent. Twenty-one poems of that collection are the core of this collection.

... to the Arvon Foundation for providing wonderfully-varied residential courses on literary themes. I was inspired by the course on *Writing and Science* given by Lavinia Greenlaw and John Latham. *Second Coming*, *Flash after Flash* and *Anatomy Class* stem from that productive week.

... lastly I thank all those who have contributed substantial critiques and made helpful suggestions: Joe Lyons, a friend from university days; Gordon Read, fellow MA course student; and Ian Searle, a writer and a school contemporary who renewed contact with me through FriendsReunited.

CONTENTS

LONG TIMES, LARGE NUMBERS

Cosmic Time: Linear	11
Cosmic Time: Logarithmic	11
The Supermole: a Lecture	12
Lobelia	14
Geological Drama	16
Trio of Geological Faults	20

LIFE AND DEATH

Cell Proliferation	23
Life's Dance	24
Second Coming	25
Caveman's Descendent	26
Flash after Flash	27
Flu Victims: 1918	28
On Newton	30
In Memory of Roy Edgar Meads	33
A Tribute to Bill Hamilton	36
Anatomy Class	38
Disco Trip: a Mock-epic Descent	40
Oracles	42
Ann's Song	44
Bell's Insight	45
Bye-bye, Blüthner	46

ENVIRONMENT

Watch Where You Tread	49
Desert Soil	50
It Doesn't Pay to Mess with Nature – or Does It?	52
What am I?	52
Storm	53
Marine Admonition	53
Himalayan Balsam	54
River	54
The Shepherd's Hour	55

NOTES ON THE POEMS

Notes are given for every poem, indexed by their page numbers. They are intended both to help in understanding those poems that, due to their subject matter, have vocabulary that is unlikely to be familiar to the general reader and also to set the poems in context and indicate interesting factors associated with their origins.   57

LONG TIMES, LARGE NUMBERS

Cosmic Time: Linear

14 BYa	One hundred million years per syllable
13 BYa	will trap the Universe in fourteen lines.
12 BYa	Here cosmic dust accretes to galaxies,
11 BYa	and supernovae blow themselves apart.
10 BYa	The thermonuclear furnace of the Sun
9 BYa	is commissioned in line six. More débris
8 BYa	congeals to planets: modest Mercury
7 BYa	to giant Jupiter and Saturn, ringed.
6 BYa	The sestet greets the cooling ball of Earth.
5 BYa	Iron falls to the core. Crustal plates float,
4 BYa	collide, make mountains rise. The last half line
3 BYa	has life invade the land. Three final words
2 BYa	see 'giant lizards' come and go; shrews, mice
1 BYa	and mammals thrive; and humans just squeeze in.

Cosmic Time: Logarithmic

14 BYa	Photons, electrons, galaxies and suns.
1.4 BYa	Bacteria, trilobites and trees abound.
140 MYa	The dinosaurs arrive . . . . . . few left around.
14 MYa	Mammals evolve . . . . . . *Australopithecines.*
1.4 MYa	Now *Pithecanthropus* tastes flesh, makes tools.
0.14 MYa	*Neanderthals* light fires and hunt with spears.
12,000 BC	The ice-age ends and modern man appears.
602 AD	Saxons yield to Normans . . . . . . Victoria rules.
June 1862	War, war, I'm born, war, schooled, wed, parent twice,
19 Jun 1988	grandfather now, and ageing by degrees –
25 Jan 2001	a PhD of no vocational use,
5 May 2002	this month I must get down to my MA.
15 Jun 2002	Two sonnets in a week, I'm under way!
20 Jun 2002	Time for a break, watch Countdown, eat my tea.

The Supermole: a Lecture

All grocer shops when I was young had scales
and sets of brass homunculi as weights
lined up by size, cyclopean: one ounce
to seven pounds. Long since displaced
by electronic digital displays,
they turn up now in antique shops and fairs:
desirable, designer kitchenware.

The four-ounce weight's the one
I want to talk about. Imagine that
it's melted down and cast into a cube,
not quite an inch along each edge,
and left to slowly cool. It takes the form
of a single crystal, β-brass,
copper and zinc layers alternately:
one hundred million atoms to a row;
one hundred million rows to a layer;
one hundred million layers in the cube.

So just how many atoms have we got?
A supermole! A trillion trillions!
That's ten to the power of twenty four:
1 000000 000000 000000 000000
It's unimaginably huge, it needs
eccentric counting games to give it scale
and cut it down to size. Let's make a start.

With magic tweezers, magnifying glass
and steady hands we pick the atoms off,
one every second. Our progress is slow –
more than three years to liquidate one row!
If we continue at this pace we'll take
three million cosmic lifetimes to complete!

Let's try again. We'll pair each atom with
a blade of grass – trampling each cricket pitch,
each field and meadow, hill and mountainside,
each prairie, steppe and plain around the world:
some twenty layers will disappear, no more!

We'll fare a little better if we pair
each atom with a grain of sand, go round
the coast of Britain, each blue-flagged beach from
Land's End to Land's End *via* John O'Groats.
One hundred thousand layers will go, that's like
two thicknesses of kitchen foil! To use
the whole cube up we'd need a thousand trips –
equivalent to all Sahara's sand.

Two illustrations now to get a feel
for scale in dimensions other than three:
firstly, slice it layer by layer and join
them in a fifteen acre chequered square,
enough to cover five soccer pitches;
secondly, and somewhat surreally,
join all rows end-to-end to make a thread,
the finest filament conceivable,
enough to run round every planet's orbit
with twenty-five radial links to the Sun.
You thought a spider's web was delicate!

Your challenge now will be to estimate
the storage space that Captain Birdseye needs
to hold a supermole of frozen peas.
Also you might go on to prove my law
(unpublished hitherto): there's never been
a supermole of any living thing
that's visible to the unaided eye.

The answer to the challenge is given in the end-notes.

Lobelia

My favourite lobelia
is *Erinus compacta* 'Cambridge Blue',
clear sky-blue flowers without an eye.
I grow them from Thompson & Morgan seed,
Contents approx. 2500
the packet states. Tiny, uncountable,
they barely cover my thumbnail,
weighing me down, eight micrograms apiece!

Seedsmen will put a pinch into
a drill but, for the sake of argument,
I put a *single* seed into
damp compost in a three-inch pot. I wait
a week, a thin shoot pushes up:
looks like slow creeping stealth but that's not so.

What really takes place in the dark?
Each *second* spent in that dank ambience
a *trillion* molecules pass through
the seed coat first, then root-hairs and the root.
Water, nitrates, magnesium
to start. Then, when the first two leaves unfurl,
the influx leaps a million-fold
as water from the air and CO_2
stream through each stoma in the leaves,
conspire with sunlight for a month or two:
leaves energized by photosynthesis,
all the unneeded oxygen expelled.

Out of my sight the roots extend,
soak up essential minerals, support
this miniature bonsai bush,
four inches tall. From when the blue appears
there's maybe a month of pleasure
as loss and gain of molecules
just balance out – the flowers poised
to receive the pollen-traders.

The petals wilt and drop. New seed
forms and ripens. Leaves wither, stalks and stems
stiffen, and seeds fall to the soil –
countably many from the single one
with which this verbose tale began:

the generous arithmetic of botany.

Geological Drama

Act I

4.6 BYa   A billion years of the Precambrian pass
without a sign of life. The primal sea
3.6 BYa   swirls around a single continent
whose coast will host the single cells
of life for the next two billion years.
1.5 BYa   Life in the Mesoproterozoic
masters the multicellular trick.

Interlude: Snowball Earth

900 MYa   The Neoproterozoic era
suffers life's first major catastrophe.
Disintegration of the landmass leads
to a girdle of continents around
the Equator. Once land-locked areas
are now exposed to ever-increasing
rainfall. CO_2 is leached from the air
and global cooling commences. Ice forms
at the poles and glacial fingers grow
to grasp the entire globe. Oceans freeze
and ninety-five per cent of species die.
A few survive near hydrothermal vents.
Volcanic action turns the climate round:
magma melts ice and levels of CO_2
increase a thousand-fold – global warming
rules, temperatures rise. Marine life spreads
again – a myriad forms created
in genetic isolation.

Act II

544 MYa   Life in the Palæozoic era
burgeons, diversifies. The Cambrian tells,
530 MYa   through the Burgess shale, of the explosion
of forms, of the first hard-bodied creatures,
of oddball species (most of which died out
like *Wiwaxia*, a sea-bed scavenger,
five-eyed *Opabinia* and the giant
Anomalocaris, three feet in length)
and of the first known chordate, *Pikaia*,
which *did* survive, else we would not be here.

505 MYa	In Ordovician shales the first fish fossils are found and in Silurian
440 MYa	limestone the first land animals appear.
410 MYa	Devonian rocks are grits and slates, shales and sandstone. Lamp-shells and corals abound.
360 MYa	Forest and fern decay to form the coal seams of the Carboniferous, molluscs, insects, sea-lilies and amphibians, too. The Permian has the New Red Sandstone, with its red marls and conglomerates, and the magnesian limestone, dolomite. All the while a great north-south divide, an entire ocean, Iapetus, contracts. Volcanic rock and muddy sediment crumple into the Caledonides. Gradually the scattered continents
350 MYa	rejoin to form Pangæa. Great reptiles roam the land – sabre-toothed gorgonopsians and their rhino-sized prey, the pareiasaurs and dinocephalians – though not for long.

Interlude: Fireball Earth

251 MYa	The Palæozoic ends in violence. Volcanoes in the Siberian Traps, not cones but a vast system of fissures, erupt for nigh on half a million years. The atmosphere is filled with CO_2, the temperature rises. Methane hydrate reservoirs, trapped beneath the coastal crust, vaporize. Great bubbles of greenhouse gas pollute the oceans and the atmosphere. Plants and plankton die off, oxygen thins and once again it's ninety-five percent of life wiped out. No trilobites remain. A single species of ammonite lives on. All other species that survive are but a poor reflection of what lived before: some thin-shelled molluscs needing little food, the 'living fossil' *Lingula* in its shallow burrow and, of course, some chordates. The Mesozoic starts in disarray.

Act III

245 MYa   Pangæa changed the weather of the world:
deserts expanded and the seas dried out,
salt spread from horizon to horizon.
Some reptiles adapted to this arid
land, their cold blood revelling in the heat.
Elsewhere, in inconspicuous places,
small, insect-eating, scuttling mammals throve.

150 MYa   Early in the Triassic, Pangæa
splits apart. Like rats on rafts the mammals
are carried away in a dozen insulations.
The first flowers bloom and in the oceans
new photosynthetic algae evolve,
the silica-secreting diatoms.
The Bunter sandstone and the Keuper marl
are largely unfossiliferous rocks.
Not so the Jurassic beds: the Lias
(a fossil of quarrymen's dialect),
where shale and limestone alternate, and the
oolite limestone (textured like fish-roe)
are packed with the remains of crocodiles,
turtles, plesiosaurs and dinosaurs.
The Cretaceous heralds ever more life:
sea-urchins, sponges, fish, strange ammonites
in the ocean; primitive types of bird
in the air; evergreen trees on the land
and the monstrous reptiles, too.

65 MYa   But then, quite suddenly, they disappear.

Interlude: Asteroid Impact

The evidence for this catastrophe
lies in a narrow band of clay between
the Cretaceous and the Palæocene.
Smaller and fewer foraminiferans
above the clay hint at extinction.
An unusual layer of carbon soot
indicates extensive forest fires.
Nine parts per billion of iridium
nest in the clay, and are not found elsewhere.

>   This is the favoured scenario:
>   an asteroid, larger than Everest,
>   smashes into the sea at Chicxulub.
>   A red-hot plume of débris shoots upward
>   and outward, and within an hour a part
>   descends on the other side of the Earth.
>   Another part goes halfway to the Moon
>   and three or four days later re-accretes.
>   The Earth rotates beneath these blasts of heat
>   and all its forests catch alight. Fifty
>   percent of animals and plants become
>   extinct, and only the smallest survive.

Act IV

65 MYa	In the Cainozoic era the Earth
	cools and mammals triumphantly evolve.
1.8 MYa	The Pleistocene promotes the primitive
300 TYa	prosimian to man in Africa.
80 TYa	From eighty thousand years ago *Homo*
	sapiens migrates, he populates
	every habitable environment.
	Since then he has mastered stone and iron,
	gone from skin-covered gourd to rock guitar,
	from cave-painted bison to Guernica,
	peered into the atom, jumped on the Moon,
	built cities on fault lines, invented war,
	sucked oil from the sand, polluted the air,
	and made possible this unfinished play.

Trio of Geological Faults

A normal fault

A *normal* fault ↘ hades to the *down-throw* –
stems from a force   that wrenches rocks apart.
Sometimes the throw is   but a foot or so,
sometimes the rock   -beds cleave and separate
by miles in a violent upheaval.

A reverse fault

A *reverse* fault ↖ hades to the *upthrow* –
stems from a force produced by compression
The rock-beds snap, broken ends overlap.
The *hanging wall* grinds over the *footwall*,
and friction polishes the *slickensides*.

An overthrust

Thin upper layers of the Earth's crust may
form an *overthrust* if sideways stressed;
and if the force is not thereby reduced

... another,   another,   and   another,   ...

may manifest as an *overthrust belt*.

LIFE AND DEATH

Cell Proliferation

The inner chamber of a temple:

a habitation for a recluse;
a cubicle for devotional use;
a cabal of conspirators;
a place to pen malefactors;

a source of electrical energy;
a region of mobile telephony;
a location on a spread sheet;
a memory unit holding one bit;

a compartment of a honeycomb
and, his analogy, Hooke's chosen term
for the minute cavities in cork, first seen
in his microscope, that's come to mean

a building block in all that's viable.

Life's Dance

Ced with Gwen
and Tom with Anne
have all been at it
since life began.

Hundreds of pairs
of just these four
line up to form
a vital gene.

A thousand genes
will likewise link
and intertwine:
a chromosome.

Just twenty-three
in sperm or egg
and forty-six
in other cells.

What follows now
is mass divorce,
new partners taken
by each base.

But Ced weds Gwen
and Tom weds Anne,
the cycle starts
yet once again.

Second Coming

You gained the dubious glamour
that extinction confers
in Amsterdam on August twelfth,
eighteen eighty-three:
became a legend in Cape Colony.
The last of your kind
now stand stuffed in museums.

It will only take a scalpel
to excise some tissue,
draw out the DNA
and implant a changeling ovum
in some unsuspecting beast:
maybe a zebra, maybe a horse.

And then we'll wait
for an uncertain gestation;
wise men, but not kings,
will attend the miraculous birth.

There's no one alive now
who remembers you
first time round –
no one to greet your *Where am I?*
with a *Nice to see you back, Quagga,
you old, rough beast!*

But no slouch, though.

Caveman's Descendent

Once Upon a Time in the West
a hunter-gatherer was laid to rest
in a chamber near a deep cave,
an important man, to judge by his grave.
One hundred years ago his stay
was rudely interrupted when, one day,
an archæologist's steel pick
let light into nine thousand years of dark.

Then *Cheddar Man*'s new home became
the Natural History Museum.
He was admired and looked upon
as Britain's oldest complete skeleton.
After a further hundred years
a professor of genetics appears,
caught in a scholarly battle
that the caveman's DNA may settle.

From a near-perfect set of teeth
the pulp cavity of a molar tooth
provided enough DNA
to get his analysis under way.
A young TV producer spots
a programme opportunity. *Why not
test some local people to see
if any share his ancient ancestry?*

A score of staff and pupils at
the secondary school are keen to let
skin cells be taken and the hunt
is on then for a living descendent.
The match is unequivocal:
Adrian Targett's mitochondrial
DNA and *Cheddar Man*'s
share common maternal inheritance.

It's a doubly satisfying story
as Adrian is Head of History,
and Targett is the perfect expression
of Nominative Determinism!

Flash after Flash

for John Latham

The lightning strikes unseen.
Amino acids spice primæval broth.
Three billion years of microbes lead
to nematodes, fish, reptiles, mammals, man.

The lightning strikes again.
The forest flames. Thoughts, flickering, form
in Logi's mind. One day he'll have
warmth and cooked meat, protection for his cave.

The lightning strikes again.
The leg of the dissected frog, nailed to
Galvani's wall, twitches in sync.
He twigs the muscle's an electric act.

The lightning strikes the brain
of Franklin (in a figurative sense).
A kite and key show how to tame
the storm, leave fragile roofs intact.

The lightning strikes between
the copper tips of an induction coil,
a small potential's multiplied
to many kilovolts across the gap.

The lightning strikes between
electrodes in a tank. From Miller's mix
of simple molecules a soup
is brewed, glycine and alanine produced.

Flu Victims: 1918

Avian viruses have been around
millions of years, no trouble to their hosts,
but when they hitch a birdshit lift to pigs
they meet an immune system that requires
them to mutate in order to survive.

A hungry US soldier eats a chop,
the swine 'flu virus takes another trip,
it's lethal in his lungs, infection spreads
from his cough's aerosol, his body drowns
in its own fluid, turning a shade of blue.

Fit-seeming soldiers, unwitting carriers,
embark for European battlefields.
A few of these will meet young Phyllis Burn,
who drives a Red Cross ambulance in France,
bussing the gassed and broken soldiers back
to hospital in the last months of war.
She knows this place of suffering and pain –
row upon row of huts, the 'nightingales',
the surgeons, orderlies, the stretchers borne
along mud tracks onto the final trench.

The end of war in sight, she travels home
to Strawberry Hill. One day of rest and then
the fever stirs. To spare her family
she moves to lodgings a few streets away
and dies within the week. It is the peak
of the pandemic with many buried
in cardboard coffins or old newspapers,
but Phyllis's mother has her body laid
in a lead-lined coffin and placed beside
her father in the family vault.

Eighty years on, virologists are keen
to enter this, now desecrated, tomb
in a quest to sequence the swine flu's genome,
to suss out the source of its virulence.
They hope to find the undegraded virus,
eight genes intact, coding for ten proteins,
in Phyllis's lung. Reverse genetics
will lead to vaccines that can be used
to thwart the agent of mass destruction
that epidemiologists agree
is only a matter of time away.

On Newton

His life and work have fascinated me
ever since I learnt we shared a birthday!
I read recently he probably suffered
from Asperger's syndrome, that he had an
'extreme male brain' as Baron-Cohen puts it,
a man who is high on systematics,
a loner, poor at communication,
and someone rather low on empathy.

I'd like to examine the evidence,
the systemizer first. This is the man
who focused on Copernicus, Kepler,
Galileo and Descartes, extracting
relevance and distilling principles
of marvellous simplicity. He wrote

> *A body stays at rest or continues*
> *in uniform motion in a straight line*
> *unless it is acted on by a force.*

> *A body's rate of change of momentum*
> *varies as the force that acts upon it.*

> *The actions of two bodies, the one upon the other,*
> *are equal in magnitude and opposite in direction.*

> *Two bodies attract one another*
> *with a force that is proportional to*
> *the product of their masses and inversely*
> *as the square of the distance between them.*

three laws of motion, one of gravity,
which, when mathematized, told the *How* of things.
Planets and tides, comets and falling fruit,
are all bound by the same four sentences:
inferences based on observation,
enquiry freed from Aristotle's *Why.*

He held that some of his discoveries,
in optics, mathematics, mechanics,
cosmology, could safely be disclosed,
becoming 'public doctrine', while others
would be too dangerous to bruit abroad,
remaining the unpublished fruit
of 'private pursuit'.

Newton the loner is the alchemist.
He disdained *vulgar chymistry* and chose
a more subtile secret & noble way of working:

subtile   is the nature of the diffuse
vegetable spirit pervading matter
and activating processes of life,
growth and material transformation;

noble   in that the alchemist would come,
through his mastery, to share God's power;

secret   so that this sacred power should not
be exposed to the eyes of the vulgar.

Part of each Cambridge year he worked that way.
As his young assistant would later write:

> *about 6 weeks at Spring & 6 at ye fall*
> *ye fire in ye Elaboratory*
> *scarcely went out*

and, though the two took turns
at tending the furnace by night and day,

> *what his Aim might be, I was not able*
> *to penetrate into.*

There is no hint of close relationship,
no wife, no mistress – systems the only
seducers. A four-year friendship at fifty
with the young Swiss mathematician
Nicholas Fatio de Duillier
appears to be the warmest that he had.

Was it coincidence that when he left
Newton suffered much mental distress?
Or was that due to breathing mercury
over a long period? Neurotic,
suspicious, he held grudges against those
that he thought menaced his reputation:
Hooke, who claimed credit for gravity's law,
lost the epithet *Clarissimus* between
the writing and the publication of
Principia; and when Hooke died his portrait
mysteriously vanished from the walls
of the Royal Society, the very
year that Newton became its President!
Empathy I'd rate as non-existent.

I find no evidence that can dismiss
Baron-Cohen's startling hypothesis.

In Memory of Roy Edgar Meads
(1929–1999)

My fingers lightly pressing the surface
of the coffin, I fight a tightening throat,
reluctant to refer to notes I hold
in my other hand, and yet hoping not
to distort or overlook some detail
expected by the first and second wives,
the two sons, cousins, colleagues and old friends
who fill St. Matthew's church.
                                          To them I say:

Roy was a long-awaited, much-loved son,
nurtured, encouraged in his early years,
bright in school subjects, musical as well.
His science flourished at High Pavement School,
piano led to organ and a life-long
passion for the music of the church.

Three years an Oxford scholar, proud to gain
a first in Physics, 'quite the best that year'.
Three more to measure the neutron's half-life
and earn the right to don the scarlet robes.
A post-doc contract in the Clarendon
got him a room, office and lab combined,
where he could give tutorials and log
emissions from excited nuclei.

He was no single-minded scientist
but sang in the Bach Choir, joined chamber groups,
was organ soloist in a Handel
concerto, publicly performed. Then from
Cambridge came his nemesis, the mighty
Wilkinson (eighty papers in ten years!)
together with his acolytes. I guess
that's why Roy failed to get a Fellowship,
and why his contract ended, unrenewed.
By then he'd wooed and wed Susan – what should
he do? Make a career in music? No!
Go schoolteaching? Another no! And then
a post was advertized at Exeter:
Lecturer required for Solid State.

*Successful candidate, he had to find
a place to live, and came to Cheriton,
to Apple Tree Cottage. Some here know why:
it boasted the first sitting-room he'd seen
that could accommodate his Steinway grand!
It wasn't long before he was installed
as organist, here in this church, a rôle
that lasted till two years ago. His sons
Christopher and Andrew were born.*
                                    *At work
he ran the Mössbauer group for many years,
joined by some here, and many a student gained
a PhD under Roy's watchful eye.*

*And yet more choirs: North Creedy Choral Soc
was formed and later Roy was President
of EMS.*
           *In the early eighties
Roy and Susan parted. And it was with
Hilary, whom he later wed, that Roy
became a traveller. Europe in the
earlier years and then the USA,
or so it was planned, had diabetes
not cruelly struck him. Since the happy
evening celebrating Roy's retirement,
at which he spoke with undiminished wit
and masterly recall, there were five long
years of loss. Though music, remarkably,
hung in till near the end.*
                                  *Roy was not
ambitious for himself but supported those
he loved – reliably, persistently.
He had an impact on my life and I
will always think of him with affection.*

The Vicar's homily that follows lauds
Roy's parochial service: organist,
clerk to the council, incisive letter
writer, champion of village causes;
music director and keyboard wizard
for the pantomime.

The *Dream of Gerontius* fills the church
with intimations of mortality;
a long-time campus friend reads from St. John;
we sing *All people that on Earth do dwell*
and *Nunc dimittis* (Lord, now lettest Thou
Thy servant depart in peace...) A trumpet
and the organ bring the ceremony
to a solemn close. Slowly we process
towards the cemetery. I cast my mind
back in reflection.
                    *It gives me pride
that I knew Roy, blood-relatives aside,
longer than any here. In October
'55 we met: Tutor and Tutee.
I'd spend an hour each week, surrounded by
racks of electronics with winking lights
counting nuclear events, while Roy would
set me straight on Schrödinger's equation
or some similar esoteric beast.
Hurdles of Moderations and Finals
were easily jumped and I found myself
starting research under Wilkinson. It
did not last—after a term I quit.
I needed a job and Roy helped me find
a teaching post. Later, in '64,
he helped me back to academe. Until
I found a house I lodged* chez Meads *and whizzed
to work and back in Roy's MG. For five
and twenty years we followed different paths.
Then Roy, tired of his own pursuits, threw in
his lot with my research group, bringing us
his complementary skills and five years' worth
of fruitful collaboration.*
                    We reach
the burial ground. The grave, agape, receives
its charge. *Man, who is born of woman...
dust to dust...* Some token soil is scattered,
flowers thrown, tears shed and farewells silently taken.

A Tribute to Bill Hamilton

Bill said that genes, not individuals,
were the base units of evolution.
How stupid not to have thought of that! said
the biologists, echoing Huxley
on Darwin. 'Kin selection' underlies
genetic transmission: altruism,
that paradoxical behaviour,
is simply distributed selfishness –
a bee dies stinging to defend the hive,
but through its many kin its genes survive.

Bill claimed that metazoans and large plants
invented sex to outwit parasites
with whom they co-evolved. He also showed
that herds and shoals are shaped to minimize
their predators' success; that the wood/bark
interface is an unappreciated
nursery of insect diversity.

His final project was to analyse
the fæces of Congolese chimpanzees,
hoping to find traces of HIV
that might just nail the origin of AIDS,
but a protozoan parasite struck first
and Bill fell to malaria. As well
as proper drugs he swallowed aspirin
which attacked an ulcer, resulting in
a massive hæmorrhage. He did not heal.

Once in another distant place
he had already written how he hoped
his passing would be handled:

*I will leave a sum in my last will
for my body to be brought to Brazil
and to these forests. It will be
laid out with full security
against the possum and vulture,
just as we make our chickens secure;
and the great* Coprophanæus *beetles
will bury me. They will enter, burrow, settle
in my flesh; and in the shape
of their children and mine, I will escape
death.
       No worm for me nor sordid fly,
I will buzz in the dusk like a bumble bee.
I will be many, buzz even as a swarm
of motorbikes, be borne, beetle by flying beetle, home:
to the Brazilian wilderness beneath the stars,
lofted under those beautiful unfused elytra
we all hold over our backs. So finally I too will
shine like a violet ground beetle
under a stone.*

The will was never witnessed and he was laid to rest at the edge of Wytham Woods in Oxfordshire. Mute, but not inglorious.

Anatomy Class

for Lavinia Greenlaw

I studied here, twice weekly for a year,
in this chill room where cold cadavers lay
on slate tables. I sometimes wondered why
they willed their final remains to first-year
students of anatomy: maybe they
feared the fire or the wooden box; wanted
post-mortal appreciation; needed
to feel they would quit the world usefully.

I remember vividly our first day –
four students standing around each table:
a few, finding it disagreeable,
turned on their heels and left us straightaway
(just as Hector Berlioz, Charles Darwin
and John Keats had done, many years before);
and the rest waiting for the Instructor
to teach us procedures, keen to begin.

A person is a material thing,
easily torn, not easily mended,
she says, *which is why a life that's ended*
becomes here a resource for the living.
If you have never seen dead bodies
before you may be feeling some distress –
but I can assure you that this will pass
as your knowledge builds up through your studies.

The donor before you is your first patient,
show them the proper respect that is due.
To prevent mould, though, and preserve tissue,
make frequent use of the wetting agent.
The copies of Clemente's Dissector
and Anatomy Atlas by your table
will prove to be nearly-infallible
guides to procedure and nomenclature.

The scalpel should be deployed with restraint,
primarily to cut through skin, and placed
on the table when not in use (not waved
in others' faces as you make some point!).
Use the probe and forceps to discover
what organs hide, and cut veins with scissors.
Keep excised tissue in the containers
for cremation when the course is over.

We shall start today with the chest. Decide
which of you will make the first incision.
Then, when you're ready, cut with precision
in a continuous stroke from side to side
below the breast... Samantha volunteered
to carry out this primal invasion
of our sixty-year-old male Caucasian.
I fell in love as that red stripe appeared!

The frontier had been crossed. Suddenly
his anonymity got through to us.
We longed to know the sort of man he was,
but over the weeks, as we delved deeply,
the evidence was inconclusive:
large muscles, a normal heart, lungs tarry,
liver cirrhosis, a withered kidney –
solely his soma, the persona elusive.

A passion for people inspires Sam and me,
which is why we are back today. We went
to the Memorial Service at 10
for our late, silent patients. Later we
lunched with their relatives, pleased to hear
their stories and answer the questions they had.
We showed them the School, and in this Room I said
I studied here, twice weekly for a year...

Disco Trip: a Mock-epic Descent

His parents think that he's gone up to bed,
his homework done; a busy day ahead.
Alexis, though, is very much awake,
fired up for risks he is about to take.
He waits to hear their door shut, the TV
News come on - then, moving stealthily,
he creeps downstairs, doctors a window catch,
slips out the back, around the cabbage patch,
into the stables where his steed awaits.
He wheels the sleek black creature through the gates
and some way down the road before he dares
to mount, insert and turn the key. It fires,
it purrs, it roars, eats up the rural miles.

Meanwhile Lucia has exercised her wiles
and told her folk she'll spend the night with Jane
but waits now at the bottom of the lane,
her ear cocked for the engine tune she knows.
She hears it, low at first, but then it grows
and suddenly there is the panting beast.
She climbs behind Alexis, clasps his chest,
lays cheek to his leather back, lets her hair
define the slipstream as the speeding pair
head for the city, seeking *Pluto's Place*.
Beside the Styx they find a parking space
and follow others who have been before
and know exactly where to find the door.

Two bouncers, Serb and Russ, survey them as
they pay and have their hands stamped with a pass.
Someone's nailed a notice above the stair:
A ban on dope's in operation here.
Undeterred, Alexis and Lucia
push on down into the crowded cellar.
Hades himself is the DJ tonight,
assisted by the gods of sound and light:
Phonon provides th'hypnotic beat of drums,
the track is one of Robbie Williams'.
The lyrics tell of love made and undone,
of lust, betrayal, heartbreak, bitter pain.

He keeps his eyes on her, and she on him,
as they progress, entranced, around the room.
From *Photon*'s lamps a spectral radiance comes,
gyrating navels glisten with bright gems,
sometimes the dancers seem to have six arms
as *Strobe* traps motion into frozen frames.
They do not touch and yet they dance as one,
faster and closer as the night draws on.

Thirst drives the frenzied dancers from the floor
to where *Persephone* maintains the bar -
an Alcopop for Alex and a Coke
to cool Lucia's throat. And then it's back
to the floor for a final hour. At three
a.m. it's time for their return journey.
The cold night air is welcome as they trace
their earlier excursion in reverse.
He drops her at the bottom of her lane -
a short goodbye and then he's off again.

Lucia will slip indoors, up to her room,
*'Jane and I fell out, Mum, so I came home,
I hope I didn't wake you,'* she'll say.
It's happened before, so now it should allay
any suspicions in her mother's head.

Alexis takes the next few miles at speed,
then cuts the engine for his final glide
into the safety of the shed. The ride
has let him think about the night's events:
it's certainly been a Dis appointment,
but definitely not a disappointment.

Oracles: at Delphi...

Know Thyself - inscription on the temple wall

Koretas noticed that his goats bleated strangely
when they grazed near a certain spring. When he
approached it he was filled with a prophetic spirit.
An oracle was set up for Earth goddess Ge
though later usurped in the name of Apollo.
Men seeking guidance came for eighteen centuries.
From ancient witness one can reconstruct the scene.
The inner sanctum of the temple is sunken
and unpaved. A sweet-smelling *pneuma* issues from
a fissure in the earth. The Pythia, priestess
of Apollo, sits on a tripod above it
with a sprig of laurel in her right hand, a bowl
of spring water in her left. She gazes at this
and, speaking with an oddly altered voice, utters
her prophesies. Plutarch, himself a priest, explains
that the *pneuma* is the plectrum that Apollo
uses to pluck his lyre, the Pythia, and make
her speak.
 Œdipus came from Corinth to consult
the oracle and was horrified when she said
you will kill your father and lie with your mother.
As he was unaware of his true parentage
all efforts to avoid these acts were doomed to fail.
A roadrage incident on his journey to Thebes
left King Laius dead. Jocasta, thereby widowed,
later became his wife when Theban citizens
honoured their promise to reward the man who rid
the city of the Sphinx by solving her riddle.
Many years after, the blind seer Teiresias
explained the plagues besetting Thebes as punishment
for patricide and incest. Bitter the moment
when confirmation of his origin was brought
from Corinth. Jocasta hanged herself from the roof
of the palace and Œdipus put out his eyes
with the brooch-pins from her dress.

The modern explanation of the oracle
combines geology and pharmacology.
Greece lies on the confluence of three tectonic
plates. Seismic activity riddles her with faults.
Two intersect at Delphi just below the site
of the sanctum. Friction vaporizes the rich
petrochemical content of the bituminous
limestone and Apollo's *pneuma* turns out to be
a mixture of methane, ethane and ethylene.
The last is the sole sweet-smelling hydrocarbon
and experiments have shown that it will induce
a trance-like state when breathed in low concentration.
As it consists of hexatomic molecules
the pitch of the voice will fall, just as a diver's
rises on draughts of monatomic helium.

How strange that momentous decisions were taken
and history shaped by the obscure utterances
of a huffer!

... and in Vienna

Freud sat behind his patients, listening unseen.
They lay on the couch and spoke whatever came
into their heads, drawing up from the unconscious
their repressed memories. Time and again they told
of jealousy, the son's of the father, the daughter's
of the mother, revealing a far earlier
sexuality than society allowed.
Freud's most famous generalisation followed:
The unconscious in our psychic life is the infantile.
He called his revolutionary insights
the *Œdipus complex* thereby giving them
the gravitas of myth and an unwitting link
to giddy goats on the slopes of Mount Parnassus
three and a half millennia before.

Ann's Song

How sweet your words when I was young,
a dell unknown by upright man,
they fell so smoothly from your tongue
and I your doxy soon became.

Then with much haste and secretly
we sought the patrico and made
our urgent vows, swore constancy:
an autem-mort that night I lay.

I twined a braid of hair, a band
for you to wear about your arm,
and bring me privately to mind
if tempted by another's charm.

Each year has seen my belly swell
with kinchin mort or kinchin co:
though some years heard the funeral bell,
the coffin through the jigger go.

Across the page I watched your quill
spider to praise some gentry mort
or, in the candlelight, to scrawl
the sermon on next Sunday's text.

The law and Latin served you well
in commerce of the heart and soul,
but sixteen years of woman's toil
have worn me down, my spirits fail.

My stamps and fambles colder grow,
the flame dips and the tallow flows.
Lightmans and darkmans I loved you true.
Remember me, my glaziers close.

dell	virgin	jigger	door
upright man	chief vagabond	gentry mort	gentlewoman
doxy	mistress	stamps	legs
patrico	priest	fambles	hands
autem mort	church-wed woman	lightmans	day
kinchin mort	girl	darkmans	night
kinchin co	boy	glaziers	eyes

Bell's Insight

I have heard a ray of the sun
laugh and cough and sing!
  Alexander Graham Bell
  in a letter to his father

A sweep of the flame
removes impurities,
leaves glass, cloudy at first,
flawless and clear.

A thimbleful of silica
makes a mile of filament
to carry streams of coded light
in subterranean webs.

*

Computers crunch the data
from radars round the world:
fibres resist the crosstalk
and can't easily be tapped.

*

There in a hospital the beam
caroms through the fibre's core
scanning the roller-coaster turns
of a digestive tract.

The instrument display,
brighter than neon,
points up an imperfection
for the laser to burn out.

*

Today we can talk on a light beam,
look through night-vision goggles
at the stars, pierce through bad weather:
fog, snow, rain, smog, whatever.

Bye-bye, Blüthner

The fall was ever up – the keys
and pedals called enticingly.
Playing Schubert was purest joy,
the upper registers sang sweetly.

It was the Sunlight sonata
that played most days through the summer,
causing the rosewood case to fade
and blisters to sully the surface.

My cousin David, luthier, came
and helped me scrape the varnish off.
His resin with bee propolis
at once restored the rosewood sheen.

For a little while, all went well.
Then came the day the high notes clacked,
unpitched. Hearing-aids failed to cope,
foiled by harmonic resonance.

Another day the chords I played
were not the chords shown on the page:
macular degeneration
had set in, and cataracts too.

It had to go. So four men came
and deconstructed it, fitting
it into a customized box.
Then off they went to London.

To Conway Hall, to an auction:

**Lot 121 Blüthner No 90800
a 6ft 3in Model VIII in rosewood case
on dual square tapered legs.**

Born in Leipzig, 1913,
well-loved for nearly 50 years.

ENVIRONMENT

Watch Where You Tread

The flip-flop of the water has me jelling up
against my kin in a raft of bubble-wrap.

When the tide retreats I hope
for a stranding in a pool
where my ganglia can be tickled
by shrimp and water-fleas,
where my filaments can float
as bait to catch the eyes of those
who search for anemones and crabs.

I have a surfeit of toxin ready
to raise weals on the unwary.

Desert Soil

for David Brown

For soil read sand, and think
of the beach above the tideline:
sand that is loose, vulnerable to wind,
that spills like liquid from the hand,
a trap for the occasional seed,
if sporadic tufts are any guide.

And then forget the sea but magnify
the beach ten-thousandfold,
slope it downwards from west to east
in a gentle undulation of valleys,
where once rivers ran, and gullies,
where infrequent rain is caught.

Add some exotic plants
with tenacious roots, resisting
the winds and the sandstorms
and feeding the sheep and goats
that daylong seek them out.

Last, set the shepherd in the scene:
loose-robed, head covered but not, as in
some biblical image, bearded – being
but fourteen years of age. He hunkers down,
master of patience and the sculpted horizon.

A distant swirl of sand catches his eye,
camel and rider shimmer slowly towards him,
their image refracted through the desert heat.
This is his brother coming to say
that the flock must be taken south,
away from the invisible border;
that an army is to take its place,
awaiting an invasion order.

Their journey starts as steel behemoths
(Crusaders and Saracens their ancestors)
lumber remorselessly from the east.
Track after clanking track compacts the sand.
After a week there's not a plant alive
and it will be five years before the land
will once again allow a flock to thrive
and shepherds to return.

Meanwhile the empty cigarette
and ration packs, the Cola cans
and the spent shells of practice rounds
litter the place – are desert soil:
bitter the price of the desert's oil.

It Doesn't Pay to Mess with Nature – or Does It?

As an experiment I grew
tomatoes in an unusual way.
I trained a stem along the ground
and coaxed four sideshoots upwards
till each resembled a whole plant.

But some fruit split,
some were smaller than cherries,
and some sprouted obscene addenda.

A failure? I don't think so.
I got a certificate –

**Annual Garden Show
Class 20 : Comical Vegetable
1st Prize**

– and 50p.

What am I?

I'm a brass tambourine
with a woven-wire skin,
you take me from the shelf
and heap me from the bin.

Shaken from side to side
my charge subsides.
You keep what eludes me
but reject what I grasp.

You let me be myself!
I make the grade.

Storm

Exhilarating, wild, the sluicing rain
rattles the slates. Lightning illuminates
the darkened room, the power long since gone.

Outside the thunder thrums continuously
as fork on fork and sheet on sheet create
a filigree nearly as bright as day –

like retinal veins in that tangled skein
seen briefly as an after-image when
the ophthalmologist concludes his scan.

I venture outside when the storm retreats,
streetlights come on as the power returns.
I relish the coolness as the rain abates,

the world's thirst quenched, and entertain a dream
where Nature copies Art – with Beethoven's
Peasants merrymaking after the storm.

Marine Admonition

Beware the water's tentacles,
the hooks and eyes of the waves,
the weeds about your ankles,
the spells the coral weaves.

Think of the souls of sailors
whose bones lie in the sand,
whose ships pursued the sunset
yet never sighted land

Himalayan Balsam

I deny that I'm
an illegal immigrant,
an undesirable alien.

I just journeyed here
seeking a temperate clime
and a place where
my roots could keep damp.

Along lanes and river banks
I've tried to blend in, my purple
like toadflax and foxglove,
thistle and water mint,
my bronze stem like bramble.

I long to belong.

River

I make no sense,
washing the willow roots,
whispering white noise.

Mostly I surge repeatedly,
abrading the bouldered bed,
gurgling mindlessly.

In flood my waters rise
bloated by downpour,
breaching my boundaries,

relaxing into lakes,
leading to loss
of landscapes

and to silence.

The Shepherd's Hour

The moon is red where distant haze is dense,
And in a dancing mist the meadow sleeps
In blissful idleness, a shiver creeps
Among the rushes where a frog laments.

The water lilies fold their heads and sleep,
The rugged poplar trees stand out on high
In the far distance, vague where earth meets sky,
And all the fireflies to the bushes keep.

The screech owls wake, rise noiseless in their flight,
On heavy wings through darkening air they go,
Above them spreads the evening's ashen glow,
Venus emerges, white, and all is night.

The above is a translation of the following poem by Paul Verlaine.

L'Heure du Berger

La lune est rouge au brumeux horizon;
Dans un brouillard qui danse la prairie
S'endort fumeuse, et la grenouille crie
Par les joncs verts où circule un frisson;

Les fleurs des eaux referment leurs corolles:
Des peupliers profilent aux lointains,
Droits et serrés, leurs spectres incertains;
Vers les buissons errent les lucioles;

Les chat-huants s'éveillent, et sans bruit
Rament l'air noir aves leurs ailes lourdes,
Et le zénith s'emplit de lueurs sourdes.
Blanche, Vénus émerge, est c'est la Nuit.

NOTES ON THE POEMS

11   Cosmic Time: Linear

The epoch (technically a moment in time, not a period of time) before the start of each line is shown as B(illions of)Y(ears)a(go). It is not intended to be part of the poem.

11   Cosmic Time: Logarithmic

The dates at the start of the first six lines are given as B/M(illions of)Y(ears)a(go).
In the last line: I used Countdown because I was a regular viewer of the TV programme. Only weeks after writing did I realize that the word summarizes the entire poem!

12   The Supermole: a Lecture

The answer to the challenge in the last stanza: If the freezer covered the entire UK it would need to be 1600 km tall.

14   Lobelia

This poem is also a lecture on mind-boggling numbers. It is now focused on natural processes where stillness belies frenetic activity.

16   Geological Drama

The dating of periods is uncertain – different authorities assign dates that may vary by 20 or 30 million years.
In Act II: The Burgess shale is found in a quarry high in the Canadian Rockies at the eastern border of British Columbia. According to Stephen Jay Gould in his book *Wonderful Life* a single stratum seven to eight feet thick and less than 200 feet long contains more anatomical diversity than all the world's seas today.
In Act II: '... else we would not be here.' is perhaps an incorrect claim. We may have evolved from some other chordate. All vertebrates have chordate ancestry.
In Act III: The Lias is dialect word for Layers, fossilized and preserved.
Interlude: The Mayan word is pronounced cheek-shoo-loob

20   Trio of Geological Faults

In line 1 hade rhymes with fade. As a noun it denotes the angle between a fault plane and the vertical. As a verb it means dip, lean or slope. The italicized words were terms used by miners long before geologists were around. The slickensides are gleaming polished surfaces of rock that arise as a result of two strata moving relative to each other.

23   Cell Proliferation

Line 11: In 1665 Hooke published *Micrographia*, a collection of scientific observations, illustrated by his own beautiful engravings, of objects seen through the microscope. His chosen term for a basic structural unit of biological material has become universal.

24   Life's Dance

Lines 1 and 2: Each strand of the double helix that comprises deoxyribonucleic acid (DNA) is an enormous sequence of just four chemical units. Two of these are 'purines': adenosine (Anne) and guanine (Gwen) and two are 'pyrimidines': cytosine (Ced) and thymine (Tom). Disparity of size between purines and pyrimidines means that the rungs of the helical ladder consist of one of each of these classes: thymine always links with adenine and cytosine with guanine.

25   Second Coming

Quagga is pronounced KWAH-ha.

26   Caveman's Descendent

Nominative Determinism describes the cod-psychological process whereby some people acquire jobs or fulfil destinies in keeping with their names – the collaborators in animal ethology Lionel Tiger and Robin Fox, the detective Jack Sawyer, etc. It is a recurrent theme in the Last Word pages of the *New Scientist*.

27   Flash after Flash

Stanza 2: Logi subsequently became the Norse god of fire.
Last stanza: Early attempts at replicating the conditions for the emergence of life encouragingly produced a few of the necessary amino acids.

28 Flu Victims: 1918

Last line of stanza 2: Heliotrope cyanosis was a characteristic feature of this flu.
Stanza 3: Phyllis Burn returned to London in October 1918. She died on October 30th, aged 20.
Stanza 3: Her family comprised her mother and two younger sisters. Her father, Major James Burn, had died six years previously.

30 On Newton

We were both born on Christmas Day, he in 1642, I in 1934. Simon Baron-Cohen is Professor of Developmental Psychopathology at Cambridge University and the author of *The Essential Difference: the Truth about the Male and Female Brain*.

33 In Memory of Roy Edgar Meads

In the first italic section: The Oxford DPhil robe is a magnificent scarlet garment.
EMS is the Exeter Musical Society.
In the second italic section: Moderations was an examination at the end of the first year at Oxford.

36 A Tribute to Bill Hamilton

Stanza 3: HIV is the human immunodeficiency virus. A controversial theory of the origin of acquired immunodeficiency syndrome (AIDS) claims that HIV crossed from primates to humans through a tragic human error in the preparation of the oral polio vaccine (OPV). The latter was cultured in the kidney tissue of chimpanzees and the possibility exists that one of these animals was infected with a mutant version of S(imian)IV, i.e. HIV. The initial concentrations of AIDS cases coincide in times and places with massive polio vaccination campaigns involving vast numbers of Africans.
l.45 elytra are the forewings of beetles modified to form cases for the hindwings.

38 Anatomy Class

This poem began life as a reflection on the work of pathologists and their relation to the cadavers they handled. I showed an incomplete first verse to Lavinia Greenlaw in a tutorial session during an Arvon course. In discussion she revealed that her parents had met in the dissection room when medical students. I subsequently changed my pathologists into medical students and introduced a love interest. The poem is composed of eight *brace octaves*, eight-line stanzas rhyming *abbacddc*.

40   Disco Trip: a Mock-epic Descent

The *heroic couplet* is a pair of rhyming iambic pentameters. Alexander Pope wrote a number of long poems consisting of them, occasionally punctuated by a triplet. The poem here is an elaborate fantasy based on a revelation by my son when he was 30 that he had made nighttime motorbike excursions around Devon lanes when he was 17.

42   Oracles

The oracle was active from some time around 1400 BC when it was first associated with the Earth goddess, Ge, then taken over by Apollo's followers around 800 BC. It took place about once a month during the nine months of the year in which Apollo was held to be resident. It was closed by the Christian emperor Theodosius in 393 AD. Huffer is an American usage for a substance abuser.

44   Ann's Song

I was tasked with writing a poem about a woman of the 16th century. I chose Ann More, born in 1584, as my subject. She became the wife of the poet John Donne in 1601, when she was 17. I decided to incorporate some of the jargon of the Elizabethan underworld in telling her story. This was taken from the fascinating book *Cony-Catchers and Bawdy Baskets* by Gāmini Salgādo.

45   Bell's Insight

Alexander Bell's invention of the telephone, patented in 1876, was a result of his research into hearing and speech The latter was motivated by his mother's deafness and his wish to develop devices to assist the deaf. In 1880 Bell and an associate developed and demonstrated the photophone. It was Bell's insight that the telephone wire could be replaced by a light beam. This was the precursor of the optical fibre, the subject of the poem. Bell considered the photophone to be his greatest achievement.

46   Bye-bye, Blüthner

The fall is the hinged flap that covers the keys.
A luthier is a maker of stringed instruments, violins etc. Bee propolis is a sticky resinous substance collected from trees by bees and used to seal their hives. It is commonly included in the resins used by instrument makers.

49   Watch Where You Tread

Only bilateral creatures can have brains. Jellyfish have a nerve net instead of a central nervous system. This net is spread across the body and consists of sensory neurons that detect chemical, tactile and visual signals, motor neurons that detect movement in the body wall and intermediate neurons that detect activity in the former and send signals to the latter. Groups of the intermediate neurons may cluster into ganglia.

50   Desert Soil

Penultimate stanza: Crusader and Saracen were the names of tanks in earlier wars.

52   It Doesn't Pay to Mess with Nature – or Does It?

The subject matter prompted me to write a poem in an unusual way.

52   What am I?

I'm a coarse sieve, namely a riddle!

53   Storm

The penultimate movement of Beethoven's Sixth Symphony contains a vivid evocation of a storm. Its last movement is headed *Peasants merrymaking after the storm.*

53   Marine Admonition

The opening of this brief poem was suggested by some images in Japanese painting.

54   Himalayan Balsam

This poem and the next resulted from a nature walk undertaken to gather ideas for poetic treatment.

54   River

See previous note. In recent times there have been floods in Yorkshire and Somerset which have left hundreds homeless for many months.

55   The Shepherd's Hour

In France the planet Venus is referred to as *le Berger*, the Shepherd. The relative positions of the Earth, Venus and the Sun are such that Venus can be seen from Earth only in the hour before sunset or the hour after sunrise.